I0420753

"THE 2050 INITIATIVE"

BY

MARK CARVEN OLDS, MNO, CNM, CPE

To some, 2050 may seem an extreme distant year, nevertheless, procrastination can eat up a half-century without anything positive having been accomplished. "The 2050 Initiative" shall set forth a detailed plethora that must begin immediately to reach a broad positive outcome that will inspire an entire people within the span of a single generation.

1

"The 2050 Initiative" ought to summon the brightest minds and the most abundant resources available to Black People to engage in the production of resolves, resolutions, and solutions. *"The 2050 Initiative"* will invoke plans for positive actions beyond mere discussion without strategic mobility. To attract talented and skilled laborers, *"The 2050 Initiative"* will bring into being programmatic endeavors that shall transcend academic researchers or vaunted political orators.

On the march toward the outcomes sought for achievement by the year 2050, *"The 2050 Initiative"* must set forth attainable benchmarks. *"The 2050 Initiative"* shall set the battle array to heal the current generation as well as to deliver total liberation to the next generation. The Black babies born in 2025 should come into a nation with the resources already set aside to fund whatever their destiny and vision can determine as total freedom. These 2025 babes will only need care and nurture in order to make an entrance on the passageway of ascendancy to visionary leadership set for 2050.

Mark Carven Olds, MNO, CNM, CPE
Managing Director, Midwest Minority Think Tank

DEDICATION

To the beloved memory of

Willie Grey Olds
And
Ida Mae Wilkes Olds

"THE 2050 INITIATIVE"

MARK CARVEN OLDS

Copyrights 2015

TABLE OF CONTENTS

SECTION III

Introduction:

"**T**he 2050 Initiative**"** will present the vision of where Black People, African-American descendants of African slaves living in America, shall occupy collectively in areas of culture, economics, education, politics, sociology, and theology in the Year of Our Lord 2050 A.D. *"The 2050 Initiative"* shall exceed any sociopolitical manifesto. This interchange can bring to pass an inoculation for Black People against failure or desolation. **"The 2050 Initiative"** shall also serve as a vaccine that will declare preparation as the means to overcome any hurdle or obstruction. In addition, "The 2050 Initiative" shall build up the immune system of a people to conquer the fear of failure, while rejecting an inactive complacent inclination. **"The 2050 Initiative"** will thrust forth an active agenda. This proactive agenda has been birthed by the Spirit and shall spread from breast to breast among Black People.

To some, 2050 may seem an extreme distant year, nevertheless, procrastination can eat up a half-century without anything positive having been accomplished. *"The 2050 Initiative"* shall set forth a detailed plethora that must begin immediately to reach a broad positive outcome that will inspire an entire people within the span of a single generation.

Impactful change for a people must begin with the commitment of elders who will most likely not live to see the realization of the vision. Such an exertion by the elders

7

of Black People would symbolize an unselfish spirit bent on building for others what is inherently good. In the midst of this contemplative series of actions, these foresighted elders shall possess a cognitive recognition that a personal taste of the outcome aspiration may never occur. In spite of this probable life expiration likely reality for most of the elders involved, this action shall constitute the epitome of released compassion and the paragon of passion for an unselfish cause.

God has the power to inevitably preserve two, three, or more witnesses to confirm His plane of Divine history among humanity.

"The 2050 Initiative" ought to summon the brightest minds and the most abundant resources available to Black People to engage in the production of resolves, resolutions, and solutions. *"The 2050 Initiative"* will invoke plans for positive actions beyond mere discussion without strategic mobility. To attract talented and skilled laborers, *"The 2050 Initiative"* will bring into being programmatic endeavors that shall transcend academic researchers or vaunted political orators.

On the march toward the outcomes sought for achievement by the year 2050, *"The 2050 Initiative"* must set forth attainable benchmarks. *"The 2050 Initiative"* shall set the battle array to heal the current generation as well as to deliver total liberation to the next generation. The Black babies born in 2025 should come into a nation with the resources already set aside to fund whatever their destiny and vision can determine as total freedom. These 2025 babes will only need care and nurture in order to make an entrance on the passageway of ascendancy to visionary leadership set for 2050.

King David was not permitted by God to erect a sanctuary.   That distinctive honor was reserved for the next generation builder. However, King David refused to pout; instead, he gathered all the resources as well as the strategic alliances that a youthful King Solomon would have need of to accomplish the vision. As a result, a historical edifice arose which no temple has ever been able to match the splendor and the majestic aura of King Solomon's Temple.

"The 2050 Initiative" shall define an accumulative conglomerate of the current living Black People as the "Prophetic David" and the younger generation of Black People as the "Prophetic Solomon."   These two generational types shall mesh to bring about the redemption and salvation of a people. The King, David, penned from his prophetic office as a Psalmist, "O God, You have thought me from my youth, And I still declare Your wondrous deeds. And even when I am old and gray, O God, do not forsake me, Until I declare Your strength to this generation, Your power to all who are to come." {Psalm 71:17,18}

"The 2050 Initiative" will introduce five key expressions as essential to move a people toward a vision. These five key expressions cannot become construed as a panacea. In spite of that, these pivotal assertions shall act as the flurry of pursuits before the perfect storm of progress.   Such strategic exploits set in motion shall constitute measures potent enough to fuel and ignite a movement.

Within *"The 2050 Initiative,"* a significant message (five key expressions) shall reveal measures that will expound upon:

*Black Global Equivalence
*Black Social Order Reconstruction:
   Domestic Realignment
*Black Voters: Free Agency
*Black Youth Rediscovery
*Stop the Black Cannibalism

The full emancipation can only begin with an internal judgment that shall inspire rather than condemn. *"The 2050 Initiative"* should look to shake up the people without shattering their spirit. Black People must have an incentive to gear up, in order to face such an all-inclusive moral challenge. This provocation should displace comfort while planting the seed of creative tension.

The Prophet Jeremiah faced a similar dilemma in pass millenniums. His people were on the crevice of eradication. His people stood along a narrow fissure as *"The 2050 Initiative"* will confront with this coeval generation of Black People. Stagnation by a crack, a people will eventually cave under the weight of the mass. The end result will lead to a people falling into a vast chasm. A prophetic voice, such as Jeremiah, will see an opening that can support a multitude who may march in rank to the safety over an illuminated passageway.

The following words came to Jeremiah's defining moment, "Then the Lord stretched out His hand and touched my mouth, and the Lord said to me, 'Behold, I have put My words in your mouth. See, I have appointed you this day over the kingdoms, To pluck up and to break down, To destroy and to overthrow, To build and to plant.'" {Jeremiah 1:9,10}

*Black Global Equivalence

"The 2050 Initiative" shall acknowledge and recognize the monumental accomplishments and the achievements of individuals. Such achievements have often been a historical credit to the Black race. However, individual attainments have not been able to transition into Black Global Equivalence. *"The 2050 Initiative"* must take aim at uplifting the collective body of Blacks.

"The 2050 Initiative" shall reveal solid steps to mobilize an entire people. "The 2050 Initiative" has no interest in revisiting an affirmative action battle, nor the announcement of a fresh round of elaborate entitlement programs. Within the Black Global Equivalence, three significant outcomes shall come forth by the execution of this exertion:

1) Black Worldwide Equality,
2) Black Comprehensive Interaction Acceptance Virtually Identical to all other People on the Planet, and
3) Black Far-Reaching Evenhandedness.

*Black Social Order Reconstruction: Domestic Realignment

"The 2050 Initiative" will address succinctly the immediate need to launch a systemic Black Social Order Reconstruction. With a specific attention paid to Domestic Realignment, family structure shall head the list to move a people in that direction. To become productive citizens in the broader society, the accountability and responsibility of the family must have a formal context as established core values. Obedience to parents (authority) and respect for elders (spiritual leadership) must return as core values which should first have inauguration within the home setting.

Individual gains should receive applauded status; however, there must emerge a complete strategy geared toward the upward mobility of the millions rather than the successful thousands. No need shall exist for the further exhaustion of time on the analysis or the study of difficult conditions. By now, the statistical data has been well documented. *"The 2050 Initiative"* shall enthusiastically salute the thousands and will fervently implore them to assist the millions in the establishment of:

1) Black Sequence Positioning: An Internal Set,
2) Black Communal State Configuration: An Inner Posture, and
3) Black Interactional Dispositional Arrangement: A Central Germaneness.

*Black Voters: Free Agency

"The 2050 Initiative" shall diligently advocate the educational and radical invoking of the right to vote. The use of the vote must undergo radical, intellectual, and strategical revision practice. Black voters must become a forceful action of creative tension; rather than, a (stumbling) voting bloc that has been destined to a foregone conclusion of a single party dominance.

In the electoral process, the Black voters' ballot count on local issues and matters centric to Blacks should have an identifiable numerical presence. On the other hand, candidates, who have not aggressively demonstrated an open support of Black causes or issues, should not presume a favorable heavy Black voter turnout.

As an alternative to candidate loyalty, issue campaigns should have the primary focus of Black voters. This is a particular area where Black voters can best exert their collective influence. Candidates should not feel that they have an automatic entitlement to a single Black vote, when they do not identify with and support Black issues. The ideological platform of a political party ought not reign as or become the Black People's Mandate. *"The 2050 Initiative"* will call for a selective voting bloc by an enactment of:

1) Black Ballot: Independent Activity,
2) Black Enfranchisement: Nonaligned Force, and
3) Black Right to Declare: Autonomous Power.

13

* Black Youth Rediscovery

"The 2050 Initiative" shall seek to build a systemic investment in the Black Youth. A movement has to occur that can transcend boundaries of the programmatic to reach the inner sanctums of the psyche to foster a fresh orientation. *"The 2050 Initiative"* shall set forth an energetic strategy to expose multiple Black Youth to a robust positive path that may lead to success, while assertively sheltering them from the negative cultural and societal pitfalls. This shall come into existence through the systematic order of events established by *"The 2050 Initiative."*

Through a strategic advancement, "The 2050 Initiative" shall deliver a purposeful display of:

1) Black Young People Recognition,
2) Black Freshness Realization, and
3) Black Younger Generation Pioneering.

*Stop the Black Cannibalism

"The 2050 Initiative" will embrace the assignment that may influence multitudes and can cut short the rapid perpetuation of self-hatred as a community fruit. Black Cannibalism must cease and desist from devouring potential, possibility, or hope. "The 2050 Initiative" shall open a passageway to:

1) Halt Black Self-Destruction,

2) Put an End to Black Self-Ruin, and

3) Bring to a Close Black Self-Collapse.

SECTION I: "SITUATION"

"SITUATION:"

*Black American Globalization Consortium
(A harmonious agreement that has been formed to undertake a large enterprise)

Black Americans have a need to unite their economic consumer power with an international model. The effort should include multiple entrepreneurial exertions. The main focus should build a consortium that will represent the people and not as a select few individuals of color who have achieved a degree of personal success.

Black Americans must take a proactive role in the development of the increasingly integrated global economy. Black Americans cannot afford as assignment as forty million by-standers. Progress will not come to those who assume the position of an eyewitness to economic advancement on a world scale. A non-participant will become a dependent consumer, subject to the choices and decisions made by others.

The key factors to a meaningful Black American Globalization Consortium will commence with domestic unity. Commitment and trust will head the list of salient factors geared toward Black American unity. First, a full commitment to the economic support base, an increased number of commerce endeavors must materialize. Second, mistrust among Black Americans of one another has to cease as a general consensus. Trust has to overcome investment reluctance and obstructionist behavior patterns.

It will require a harmonious agreement. One that has been formed to undertake an enterprise capable of impacting the methodical practices that industries employ. Especially, the business model deployed in business transactions directed toward Black Americans.

*Black American Reparation: The Terms Thereof
(A compensation to make amends for the collateral damages, post slavery impairments, and lack of opportunity for equal access to land and natural resources)

It is a widely known fact that the United States government failed to fund the Congressional Bill which became Federal Law that would have awarded each freed slave forty acres of land a mule. That would have been the less costly approach to Black American Reparation. As a result of none funding of the legislation, Black Americans exited slavery with a tradition that would come to symbolize future political assessment. This constituency would receive symbolic gestures while other Americans would become recipients of tangible opportunities.

White America and the American government must do more than issue a symbolic apology and a statement of regret read into the Congressional Records over the misdeeds of Black slavery on its shores. The forty million plus Black Americans living in America should have a compensation awarded that could somewhat amend for the collateral damages as an aftermath of slavery. Post slavery impairments have been almost as vicious as the slavery institution itself. This can be clearly seen in the lack of opportunity for equal access to land and natural resources.

The forty acres would have proven more than a start to carve out a meager sustainable existence. This would have represented a collective potential to build an economy based upon minerals and natural resources present in the earth. The United States Government and the States that made slavery legal still have massive land holdings. Compensation dialogue should start at this level for redefining Black American Reparation.

*Removal of social barriers and ethnic prejudices that block international commerce opportunities

B lack Americans have been predominantly identified abroad by the domestic stereotypical generated imagery. The basic negative image that has been disseminated creates a reluctance to engage an independent Black American entrepreneur. As a result, Black Americans can usually find acceptance if they represent a White owned multi-national-corporation. This acceptance will come with the conventional image of an approval by some White employer.

Black Americans have standard identification as an American. They have little collective identification. This can create social barriers and ethnic prejudices that will block international commerce opportunities. This ought not to exist as hindrances for Black Americans seeking international trade opportunities.

Circumstances created nationally have preceded Black Americans. These negative bridges must become cleared. The positive image reinforcement must start on the shores of America.

Additionally, Black-Americans should embrace an international image makeover. It has become paramount that an image renaissance arises from a dedication to elevate a people.

A greater domestic Black-American entrepreneurial presence would serve as a major step to overcome categorized limitations. Labels, imposed or warranted, should be made obsolete by a careful practice of worthwhile actions.

*Black Unity in the face of the rise in populations among other minority groups in America

The diversity within the Black-American constituency does not have to construe disunity. The issues that reside at the core of concern for most Black Americans should form the unity forum. Unity should not imply one-hundred percent solidarity. However, the unity forum should represent a substantial number who agree on relative issues.

Black Unity has to go beyond tradition, exceed ideology, and transcend gulfs that divide. Economic attainment, education achievement, and religious engagement should unite Black Americans rather than create schisms. Forty million plus people should have an expectancy of variant concerns. Issues and engagement should bring enough of the Black populace together that will accomplish the desired.

In the face of the rise in population among other minority groups, Black Americans should re-think how Black Unity will be defined. With the label as the number one minority, the current definition of Black Unity has not produced an outstanding litany of recent triumphs. Contemporary years have left much to be desired on behalf of Black Americans. With the projected slide toward third minority status behind Asians and Hispanics, a new approach to Black Unity should be on the cusp.

Black Unity, more than ever, should emerge from a commonality of issues rather than mere racial solidarity.

Skin hue ought not to be the sole impetus in the quest for Black Unity. Concerns of justice, liberation, and salvation should stay as the key salient factors.

*Ineffectiveness of Black Lawmakers (Legislators):
a. local
b. state
c. federal

The ineffectiveness of Black Lawmakers (Legislators) should fall squarely upon the contemporary elected office holders. For the most part, these individuals have arisen predominantly through the Democratic Party. They most often will tow their party line and blame the Republican Party majority for their failure to produce for their constituents. If an elected official has not learned negotiation skills, then what good does holding the elected office benefit the voting bloc. More than an opposition from an obstructionist party, very few radical or revolutionary ideas have sprung forth from these Black Lawmakers.

Local: Many municipal councils have been confronted with dwindling populations, dwindling revenues, and worsening school systems. Herein will come the dilemma, a noticeable absence of creative elective officials who can make the most immediate impact, rather than a visible presence who clamor for the stage and the microphone. Ineffectiveness should not necessarily mean incompetence. Ineffective has a definition that may be an indicator of status quo entrenchment.

State: State assembly members have the lease productivity to show their constituency for their role in office. Their tenures have amounted to little more than the securing of a good job and retirement pension at the expense primarily of their constituency. Their creativity has been noticeably missing. They have provided symbolically as community leaders. The outcome or productivity has not equaled their acquired title.

Federal: The Congressional Black Caucus has the highest visibility and the lowest productivity for Black Americans. They may have delivered in a small capacity to some individuals or to a lesser degree minority organizations in their Congressional District or State. On the Federal Legislative side, they have not produced anything meaningful in quite some time, excusing a few symbolic gestures.

*Black voters blind allegiance to the Democratic Party

An African-American Democratic President, a sixty democratic majority in the United States Senate, and a democratic majority control of the United States House of Representatives, and what did that get the Black-American Constituency?

Not that the Grand Old Party has an illuminated hope to offer the Black voting bloc; however, the time has arrived for Black Americans to vote their issues. The time has exhausted for Black voters to place their ballot in alignment with the Democratic Party or any other political affiliation that will not address and deal with their issues by producing implementable solutions. In addition, Black issues cannot be decided by a political party seeking a particular candidate's election or the furtherance of a party's platform.

Black voters must decide their own issues and have a clear sense of what they expect should be a workable solution. They must learn to assemble their list of concerns and set forth their own political agenda. The concerns, issues, and proposed solutions must come from the populace and not those currently elected as office holders. Democrat, Republican, Libertarian, Green, or Independent candidate should be presented the Black voter's political agenda, which should include their concerns and issues as a viable platform. Before any potential candidate should expect to receive any nod of endorsement, he or she must declare support of the Black platform as the ticket to obtain concentrated ballot support.

The hustle of the Black vote shall end when Black voters will begin to cast their ballot for the backers of solutions to their issues and not merely personalities. This process will also end the Black voters' blind allegiance to the Democratic Party.

The question has to asked, what have you done for me lately?

*Recapturing the Unlawful
(To experience again the affirmation and the celebration of those thought to be ruined or destroyed, physically, or morally)

S piritual rejuvenation can bring about emotional healing. Then will those labeled physically or morally untouchable can find community embracing as a probability. Those thought to be ruined or destroyed cannot have community abandonment as their reality. They should have another opportunity to once again experience personhood affirmation. This will become a vital part of the foundational steps to recapturing the unlawful.

Lawlessness cannot receive a blank check from the community to operate freely. Lawlessness should not be gazed upon as an untouchable thing or acceptable behavioral institution. Lawlessness only has roots when a human being has chosen to commit an act that will violate a fellow human being. There will always be a face attached to each perpetrator of a crime. The victimizer still has connection to the human race as someone's son, brother, cousin, or former classmate.

Grandmothers have unfailingly cried out for the redemption of their grandchildren. There must also be a sensitivity to the plight of victims. Their pain cannot be ignored. The power of forgiveness can cover every aspect of any violation. The legal institutions must be allowed to perform justice through their assigned societal duties. Beyond that, the community must exercise an arm of re-

28

orientation in order to recapture the unlawful. By doing so, the cycle of lawlessness can become annihilated.

*Black-on-Black Crime or Blacks Committing Crimes Period
1) murder
2) gang, violence, recruitment, membership
3) drug sales/trafficking
4) home invasions
5) robbery
6) burglary/theft
7) rape/sexual assault
8) kidnapping
9) carjacking

Black-on-Black Crime or Blacks committing crimes period must cease. The current level of behavior in the Black neighborhoods can no longer be tolerated. Radical actions have to come forth from within the Black community. The current level of violence, disarray in the Black community is unacceptable behavior for any people.

SECTION II: "INTERVENTION"

"INTERVENTION:"

*Black American Global Presence: Black Entrepreneurs in Underdeveloped Nations
(Multiple organizers of enterprises in nations with relatively low levels of economic development)

Black entrepreneurs must take the lead in a move that will bring a meaningful Black-American presence in underdeveloped nations. Black Americans cannot achieve a global presence, if underdeveloped nations will only be left to seek aid and assistance that shall only come from the Asian or European traditional powers.

Collectively, the resources can be assembled by Black entrepreneurs. Without a doubt, the intelligence needed for successful enterprises can be found within Black Americans. The aggressiveness to create the international relations has to arrive with an economic thrust leading the way. This will require multiple organizers of enterprises of enterprises in nations with relatively low levels of economic development. These nations must be viewed as prime opportunities. The lack of a sufficient infrastructure will only add to the impact that can be realized. Through meticulous planning that will lead to great economic, social, and political stability and progress.

The presence of Black entrepreneurs in underdeveloped countries must have a mainstream image rather than a rarity presence. This occasion will represent a historical point in the economic evolution of a people.

Black-American entrepreneurs must become a part of the harvesting industry of the minerals in the earth as well as the market development of these resources.

The Black-American Global Presence must have a recognition that will far exceed that of athletes and entertainers. There has to emerge an independent economic and political advent.

*Black American Foreign Aid & the Export Thereof:
(How Blacks may render assistance to the global community)

1) Agricultural Experts,
2) Architects,
3) Computer Scientists,
4) Craftsmen,
   a. brick masons
   b. carpenters
   c. cement finishers
   d. plumbers
   e. roofers
5) Educators,
6) Engineers,
7) Medical Professionals,
   a. nurses
   b. physicians
   c. technicians
8) Researchers
9) Social Scientists, and
10) Statisticians

Black Americans must have a global connection beyond the cultural experience. The image of Black Americans has to undergo a radical transformation that shall result positive contributions to the global experience. The global community ought to receive a radically different reality of the Black American presence that what has been previously exported and perceived.

Black Americans, who may render assistance to the global community, can lift the stereotypical image that has been promoted around the globe. Black Americans have to shoulder the responsibility to force a paradigm shift. Black Americans must channel their compassion to the global community in such a fashion that the world will come to respect Black Americans as people who would rather give than take. The appearance on the global stage as equal partners will only come through well-coordinated and concerted efforts.

Foreign aid can surface from Black Americans as they present to others their gifts, skills, and talents. The export of human talent in a compassionate movement will allow Black Americans to passionately serve others. This will in turn have a significantly benevolent impact. These charitable, economic development, and sheer neighborliness will cast and portray Black Americans in an entirely different light on the global stage.

*Nation Building Series: Volumes I-V
- Nation Building: Volume I – THE PORTRAIT OF A MOVEMENT (the Transition to Nation Building)
- Nation Building: Volume II – THE PILLARS (Theology and Infrastructure)
- Nation Building: Volume III – FOUNDATIONAL DOCUMENTS
- Nation Building: Volume IV – THE PATHWAY/THE COLLAGE
- Nation Building: Volume V: PRAYER (Circumstance, Entreaty, and Supplication)

A noteworthy observation, nothing contained in the definition of a nation or Nation Building would suggest any act of violence, nor the military overthrow of another established society. Neither military aggression, nor social turbulence should represent a prerequisite for nationhood. The notable absence of an advocacy for violence should merit recognition. Nation Building that shall seek the advent of a Theological Interdependent Peaceful Society will only surface through people of faith.

A concise definition of a nation can mark a stable constituency that may sustain a social existence, which has been historically developed within a specified territory that could maintain an economic life, distinct culture, and a language in common. A nation by definition has no connection with physically destroying what already may exist. Nation Building will gather the fragmented, the imperfect, and the impoverished constituencies and mold them into a united effort. Nation Building will create a collective strength that shall demonstrate resistance to disadvantageous influences.

Nation Building shall present a pathway that will lead the fragmented, the imperfect, and the impoverished constituencies to regain dignity in a classless and a past-less society.

*The Baedeker to Nationhood
The Baedeker to Nationhood is a volume that offers clear steps which can direct a people to Nation Building

The Baedeker to Nationhood will reveal an exertion that shall be hard to accept by the political astute. Acceptance will become a more difficult visualization for those struggling with daily survival issues; nevertheless, nationhood status shall represent the viable solution for the imperfect people and the impoverished people constituency.

Nationhood shall operate outside the constraints of institutions and the limits of organizations. Nationhood shall practice inclusion of the imperfect people and the impoverished people as a unified constituency. In addition, nationhood status will enlarge the tent of the imperfect people and the impoverished people through unity with justice seekers, progressive individuals, and skilled laborers. Enlisting others, nationhood will exhibit more than an exercise in liberal conscience appeasement. Nation Building shall transcend the restrictive cultures, dogmas, and norms that have been practiced by the dominant forces of society. Nation Building will rise above the actions that have been practiced to exclude the imperfect people and the impoverished people.

The combination of existential factors, inclusive of Biblical justice, should render Nation Building practical. Nationhood status may be grasped as a concept, prayed over as a vision, and accomplished by a union of the imperfect people and the impoverished people. However, the individuals involved must commit to live in covenant and to walk by faith.

Nation Building will represent a march to collective excellence and cooperative brilliance. The Baedeker to Nationhood has captured the revelation, pointing the way to achieve by moving from idea to implementation.

*The reevaluation of the Black electorate
The Black electorate has to reevaluate its strength at the polls. The current predictable voting patterns must undergo re-assessment. Have any specific goals been accomplished? Have favored candidates delivered on promises? Does a majority alignment with a single party present the best strategy for future elections?

A voting bloc that will represent forty million plus people can certainly impact national elections. Congressional Districts and municipalities with a minority as the majority voting population have returned little to the populace in exchange for their loyalty.

Have any specific goals been accomplished?

Earlier goals may have been achieved. However the people cannot live on symbolisms. Symbolisms do not pay rent or put food on the table. Yes, a number of Blacks have been elected to office, including the highest office in the land. The value of these triumphs have a diminished value when they have been aligned alongside the multitudes in need of an improved quality of life. What are these individuals receiving in exchange for their consistent loyalty in casting ballots as directed? Past laurels might have been monumental; however, fresh goals will be necessary in order for the Black electorate to remain a relevant ballot force.

Have favored candidates delivered on promises?

This question will command the simplest answer. For the most part or anything of substance, they have not.

Skin tone or Democratic Party affiliation should no longer garner a free pass. Accountability to the concerns and issues of the Black electorate must become the measuring standard. The Black electorate must use their ballot to empower themselves and not merely one individual to an elected office. The Black electorate has to refuse the assignment of placing individuals in cushioned and secure jobs, who both forget and neglect the people responsible for their elevated lifestyle.

Does a majority alignment with a single party present the best strategy for future elections?

No. The Black electorate must vote their issues above party affiliation.

*Resurrection of creative tension as a socioeconomic or a sociopolitical tactic
The creative tension approach must come as a display that shall have an economic impact as well as a recognized political force.

Black Americans have an obligation to explore mass engagement as a means to break the malaise of non-progress. Creative tension, as a strategy, must become a proactive maneuver to break the current levels of passivity. The resurrection of creative tension will need to employ the equation of acts of civil disobedience meshed with economic re-direction and political re-alignment.

The global economy can be made to feel a significant impact from directed and purposeful spending by Black Americans. The creation of institutions that will fulfill the market demand of Black Americans can cause a significant profit margin shift.

Products manufactured by Black Americans must have access to global distribution chains. The forty million plus Black Americans would no longer be bound by the label of being consumers only. "Consumer Only" cannot exist as a sign to keep Black Americans out of participation in the global economy.

Perhaps, most visibly, the resurrection of creative tension can most easily be felt in the political arena, but will be most rapidly responded to by the economic arena.

The sociopolitical landscape can experience the immediate results of creative tension deployed by Black

Americans. The pressures of creative tension deployed by Black Americans. The pressures of creative tension can have an affect long before an election day. When issues, especially economic issues, have been clearly defined, articulated, and packaged to ascertain specific outcomes, elected officials or those hopeful of gaining an office must respond publicly. Choices will then receive a high profile, local or national.

*Recapturing the Untaught
(To educate the less scholarly and the least lettered as well as those minus formal knowledge and those without credentialed competence)

Recapturing the untaught among Black Americans, technology must not be seen as the only key to a successful future. As valuable as technology has become and will be to the future for human advancement, no adult or child should be excluded from an opportunity of self-improvement and a quality life existence.

To educate the less scholarly, the value and the image assigned to computer geeks must have an equal portrayal of craftsmen. Laborers should have respect afforded them as they master a vocational craft or skill.

The lease lettered should not be made to feel inferior. They should not have an inferior role by class distinction. Efforts, in all walks of life, ought to include a key to the uplifting of all Black Americans.

Engagement of those minus formal knowledge has to exist beyond a voter registration drive or a get out the vote rally. Recapturing the untaught must have an enduring and exhaustive approach that shall equip individuals to build economic resources.

Those without credentialed competence still may have a valid place in society. Recapturing the untaught will be an ongoing outreach to affirm the value of each Black American. By doing so, the power of the people will once again resonate in the souls and spirits of all.

Recapturing the untaught shall represent a bond that can propel respect and dignity as a core value of all humanity.

*Cease self-imposed deliberate and systematic, economic, cultural, political, and social destruction

"The 2050 Initiative" will help Black Americans cease the self-imposed, deliberate, and systematic economic, cultural, political, and social destruction. Each category mentioned has the potential (when reversed from negative acts) to assist in uplifting Black Americans.

Self-imposed has the connotation of lifestyle choices. These choices may not always infer negative behavioral patterns. The passive acceptance of status quo may eventually prove fatal for those who have been historically powerless in the struggle for systemic change.

Deliberate and systematic action can form a complicit alliance that may hinder the masses as individuals may enjoy both acclaim and profitability. Loyalty and commitment to bring forth aid to others will build a bond whereby all can experience a greater overall capacity.

The total collapse of unity will only escalate the economic, cultural, political, and social destruction. Black American unity should have a greater premium value than any point post the Civil Rights Era of the Twentieth Century. Resource access has never been high. Cultural opportunities have never before experienced global exposure. Political possibilities have exceeded projections. And finally, social mobility has exceeded all prior boundaries. Yet, the disparity of Black Americans to White American in all these categories has continually widen.

46

Oneness has to become a priority among Black Americans. Harmony in each of the aforementioned categories must be built upon the respective prevailing issue. Unity must arise from the centric core of issues and concerns relative to the causes of all Black Americans. The litany of issues and concerns will be the subject matter that will create constructive bonds.

SECTION II: "OUTCOMES"

"OUTCOMES:"

*Black American Owned Manufacturing Base
(Domestic and foreign)

"The 2050 Initiative" shall produce a Black Owned manufacturing base that has the capacity to generate multiple job opportunities and profit sharing for employees. Additionally, these plants will compose the manufacturing that shall have multiple site locations. Numerous products will come from these variant facilities. As a result of a Black American owned manufacturing base, a "true buy Black campaign" can come to full fruition. With a diversity of quality Black manufactured products, an individual would then have to make a conscious decision not to purchase a Black manufactured product.

Domestic: The Black American owned manufacturing base should consist of eight regional centers strategically located throughout the nation. These regional centers should contain a cluster of manufacturing facilities. They should produce every product that will be found in every home (i.e., iron, toaster, washing machine, dryer, trash can, silverware, china, and etc.).

The home essentials can then have personal goods such as: socks, shoes, clothing, hats, and other items.

Home building plants would also have a substantial place.

These exertions in a combined exertion would spawn multiple job creation apparatus. Fresh entrepreneurial opportunities should also arise. This would create the most substantial economic upturn in the history of Blacks in America.

Foreign: The Black American owned manufacturing base should also create the opportunity for a major replication abroad. What has been developed on American soil by Black Americans should be a part of an aggressive Black economic empowerment in other under developed nations. This paragon should prove itself to be extremely attractive. The Black American owned manufacturing base would create both import and export occasions for Black entrepreneurs.

*Black American Created Regional Entrepreneurial Centers
(Domestic and Foreign)

In addition to Black American owned regional manufacturing bases, the need will arise for Black American created regional entrepreneurial centers. The nurture and cultivation of entrepreneurs can take place in these regional centers. These centers would place individuals with fresh ideas in close proximity with available resources. From these regional entrepreneurial centers, research opportunities would become possible to assist in the development and marketing of new product lines. Moving from idea to market would no longer be an impossible dream, these potential entrepreneurs would the support of vital distribution networks and delivery systems.

Domestic: These Black American created regional entrepreneurial centers shall become an essential component of positive youth development. Economic independence from the governing system will assure that a crucial step toward independent wealth building has been initiated. These centers will harvest potential, while diverting the sub-culture lifestyles from consideration as a possible viable option. These structures that will be built along economic lines will assist in the establishment of integrity, loyalty, and trust.

Foreign: Black American created regional entrepreneurial centers will create a fresh and a positive image of Black Americans abroad. These entrepreneurial centers can cultivate local talent without exploitation as the prime motive. Rather than exploitation, the impetus of integrity, loyalty, and trust shall propel a positive image in order that Black entrepreneurs shall serve as ambassadors for all Black Americans. This overall strategy will open doors for a Black American presence in conducting import and export commerce channels.

***Black American Hemispheric Enterprise
(Commerce engagement and venture zones throughout
the Western Hemisphere)**

Black Americans have been present in the Western Hemisphere without a self-accumulative economic opportunity. Many others, individuals, corporations, and multi-national companies, have all benefitted greatly from Black American labor and ingenuity. **"The 2050 Initiative"** will call for a Black American Hemispheric Enterprise, which shall allow Black Americans to become trade partners with their neighbors.

The Black American Hemispheric Enterprise shall represent potential commerce engagement that can extend throughout North America, Central America, the Caribbean, and South America. Import and export, raw materials and finished products must have a part in the Black American trade portfolio. Black Americans shall seek trade opportunities that will provide expansion possibilities.

Venture zones throughout the Western Hemisphere shall produce the occasion for Black entrepreneurs to excel and achieve success within the Western Hemisphere. These venture zones will create opportunities for Black wares to be introduced into broader markets. Black venture zones will help establish market share, image re-definement, and investment opportunities throughout the Western Hemisphere. New opportunism will arise for Black investors. The venture zones will set in place a positive element to launch new commerce endeavors. Expansion through the Western Hemisphere by Black American entrepreneurs shall represent an ambitious directive to increase productivity within the United States by Black American owned manufacturing base.

The Black American Hemispheric Enterprise will help build a principle financial base from which entrance into the global economy shall come with less resistance. Venture zones throughout the Western Hemispheric will aid in future expansion into Africa, Asia, and Europe models.

*Reciprocity for Black Men throughout the Global Community

"The 2050 Initiative" has a goal to change any negative stereotypical images of Black men that may exist on foreign soils. Furthermore, **"The 2050 Initiative"** will raise the standard of excellence that shall become the norm of Black male expectancy. This will come forth through economic, cultural, political, social, and theological examples and practices. Ultimately, "The 2050 Initiative" will convey a distinct advantage that shall align reciprocity for Black men throughout the global community.

This will only manifest when Black men egress the White corporate structures or as agents representing the American government. There must be a vehicle that will allow Black American men to represent their own interests.

Black American entrepreneurs must be seen as representatives of Black owned commercial endeavors. It will be at this point that Black Americans shall begin to achieve global community respect. A Black American should not have to renounce his or her birthplace to demonstrate independent thinking or progressive ingenuity.

The Black cultural experience should illustrate more than an athletic or entertainment recognition. The bonds of a people should also reflect the "Collective Genius." When the males of the Black people have become respected creatively along with other external visible attributes, then reciprocity will unfold throughout the global community.

Black men must command that the issues of their people should have consideration within global political initiatives. Black Americans will be affected by global political decisions, but have been primarily excluded from any discussions. The same may also hold true for social and theological outcomes that have a global community impact.

Change in how Black men have been viewed will accelerate through **"The 2050 Initiative,"** signaling the advent of reciprocity for Black men throughout the global community.

***A New Agenda for Blacks in the United States of America
A new agenda for Blacks in the United States must originate from within**

The status quo will no longer be a viable option for Black Americans. Radical changes have arisen to the level of necessity in order to improve the quality of life for forty million plus people. The issues and concerns of Black people cannot be left to elected officials alone, nor to the conscious alignment of liberal leaning researchers.

The time has expired and portrayal no longer acceptable to have a few Black faces in high profile positions who have no policy making power, nor the moral strength to stand up for their people in the interpretation of or the development of policies. Symbolic street naming, building dedication, or statute erection will not elevate the current standard of existence. Symbolism will not bring forth economic stability to a people who have been systemically excluded from commerce opportunities.

Symbolisms and iconic figures held in larger than life esteem will not deter crime, create business opportunity, or provide housing. Food, shelter, and clothing must come through revenue generation that will provide dignity and respect. Government handouts and the multiplication of entitlement programs have run their course. Independent wealth creation, collaborative economic ventures, and social renaissance must surface for Blacks in America. A cultural renaissance shall emerge once self-hatred has been conquered through a radical collective social status uplifting agenda.

The forty million plus Black Americans may soon become the third largest minority population. Therefore, Black Americans must have a fresh view on how that will define unity among their ranks heading into the future. Skin hue, skin pigmentation, or skin tone cannot exist as the only point of solidarity. Unity ought to build issue-by-issue and concern-by-concern and not by a time cadence that actually activates procrastination. With that concept as a strategic plan, a strong platform can exist that will even allow room for differences to exist, which shall not stymie cooperative progress. For a people forty million strong, politics and religion can help, but they will not alone form a new agenda for Blacks in America. Faith, revelation, and vision will produce the season for the advent of **"The 2050 Initiative."**

"The 2050 Initiative" will construct a platform that shall be strong enough to support the well-being of all forty million plus Blacks in America.

*A Black Political Base Centric to Black Concerns and Black Issues
Black Americans cannot afford to fashion their political base on historical party affiliation. Black Americans must not feel chained to the Democratic Party out of the fear that they have no other options.

The time has arrived for a Black political base centric to Black concerns and Black issues without an isolationist posture. Inclusion in the coeval system should not automatically dictate an abandonment of the needs centric to the forty million plus Black constituents. Black Americans must have a fresh voting orientation. A vote for an issue should not command an obligation to cast a ballot for a slate of candidates. Black concerns and issues should be presented to potential candidates and not for the Black constituency to await what the candidates will present as their platform.

It must be understood by the Black voters that a well-meaning candidate may have an obvious passion for his or her party platform. This passion may carry over to include their personal heartfelt concerns; however, Black American issues may not have reached their list of priority matters. Passionate candidates may be sincere about their intent to reach the sought after office. These candidates may even be able to light a fire in the spirits of the people with passionate orations that move the soul; nevertheless, passion may not spontaneously translate into compassion for the Black concerns and issues nor reflect an iota of desire for proactive radical change engagement.

Political parties often look for centrist candidates. This will usually mean that moderate candidates may more likely be accepted by the majority of mainstream America. Again, this may have nothing at all to do with Black concerns and Black issues. A Black political base cannot become deceived by a Black candidate who may represent a political party's platform and ideology. This will not necessarily mean that this Black candidate (male or female) will represent, defend, or pursue resolve to Black concerns and Black issues.

*Black Political Free Agency
A free agent professional athlete has the most leverage after a most productive year. The free agent can then command the highest possible annual salary for the greatest potential number of years.

Black American voters have demonstrated in the last two presidential campaigns their two most productive election cycles ever. Without the Black electorate, President Obama would not have won his first term, and he certainly would not have achieved re-election for a second term.

Now will the question of Black political free agency, will Blacks stay loyal to the Democratic Party? Or, will they test the waters of the political free agency market? Blacks should not turn their ears to only hear what the candidates or parties have to state, but this the perfect season to speak into the hearing of the candidates and parties what their terms for a commitment should have as terms.

A retrospective examination of President Obama's Administration, the Democratic Party, and Black voters should undergo scrutiny. What has the Black populace actually received in return for their voting loyalty. Mostly, some symbolic emotional high of having witnessed the election of a dark skinned President. The Black community will eventually get a slew of Barack H. Obama Streets and Barack H. Obama Elementary Schools.

Black Americans should now vote their concerns and issues and not candidates with promises as fickle as the campaign literature, which most often blows in the wind. Black political free agency has become too valued to merely re-sign to a long-term contract with the Democratic Party without exploring alternatives by creating their own options.

Negotiations should open, should commence without a historical attachment. After all, the GOP can legitimately claim to be the party of Lincoln.

*Courage to be Black
Black Americans have a need for Black elected officials and organizations who still have the courage to be Black

In the Post-Racial-Obama-Political-Ear, it has become politically correct to state a philosophical and political correct position that will represent all Americans. In other words, there will be no catering to or considerations given to special interest groups (if you can believe that quote). This assessment has further established the position that an end result will produce an America where all the citizenry will prosper and be better off. Somewhere in the midst of this desired utopia will still loom the fact that all Americans have never shared the same concerns and issues. Special interest shall always be the key to balanced and equitable representation. Special interest should not carry a negative connotation.

The storybook political franchise has not worked well for most Black Americans. The last "Hope" and "Change" has not serve most Black voters too well. A quick revisit to the special interest group theme should be in order. During election cycles, it will be perfectly all right to court the Black special interest group. It will only be after the election tabulations have been confirmed that Black voters will return to their status as a taboo special interest group.

Since political mainstream America will continue looking for the most electable centrist candidate, Black-American voters should look for leaders who have the courage to be Black.

*Recapturing the Unprotected
(To preserve in a permanent form a community haven for the supervision and support of the smaller and the weaker)
(The consequence of constructive measures)

"The 2050 Initiative" will help pave the way for the recapturing the unprotected (Black women, children, and seniors). All the efforts that have been defined through this endeavor ought to preserve in a permanent form, a community haven. This community haven should provide supervision and support of the smaller and the weaker.

Recapturing the unprotected should come as a consequence of constructive measures. Black women and children should not be sexually exploited or victimized. Black elders should not be terrorized or preyed upon. And finally, Black men should not be pawns for drug cartels and prison populations.

"The 2050 Initiative" has outlined the corrective measures that shall be essential to assist in bringing forth a peaceful coexistence among Blacks and Blacks with others on the shores of America as well as the global community.

* Stop with Self-Inflicted Genocide

The following will be aim and goal of "The 2050 Initiative." A successful deploy of the proactive steps of "The 2050 Initiative" should reveal the outcomes below:

1) end to illegal drug use,
2) end to births outside marriage,
3) end to teen pregnancies,
4) end to abortions,
5) end to Black inmates in the prison populations,
6) end to the absence of marketable skill sets,
7) end to self-hatred,
8) end to education dropouts,
9) end to miseducation,
10) end to dependency upon entitlement programs,
11) end to narcissistic lifestyle practices, and
12) end to materialistic way of life.

<u>"SUMMARY:"</u>

*Benchmarks 2016:

*Benchmarks 2042

*Benchmarks 2020:

*Benchmarks 2044

*Benchmarks 2025:

*Benchmarks 2046

*Benchmarks 2030:

*Benchmarks 2047

*Benchmarks 2035:

*Benchmarks 2048

*Benchmarks 2040:

*Benchmarks 2049

"NOTES:"

The full emancipation can only begin with an internal judgment that shall inspire rather than condemn. "The 2050 Initiative" should look to shake up the people without shattering their spirit. Black People must have an incentive to gear up, in order to face such as all-inclusive moral challenge. This provocation should displace comfort while planting the seed of creative tension.

Mark Carven Olds, MNO, CNM, CPE
Managing Director, Midwest Minority Think Tank
Phone: 216.389.4340
Email: mcolds49@gmail.com

Mark Carven Olds has evolved as a sage voice of leadership in the African-American community and beyond. His emergence and resurgence has been spurred by a unique fusion of multifaceted life experiences. He has procured a viable presence in the academic, faith, and political environs.

He has earned a Master of Nonprofit Organizations degree from Case Western Reserve University, Cleveland, Ohio. He has also done post graduate studies at Case's History Department. He has also done doctoral studies at the Union Institute & University in Interdisciplinary Studies with a Specialization in Public Policy/Health, Cincinnati, Ohio. He has always and will continue to strive for fresh plateaus that may enhance the quality of life for all humanity.

Mark Carven Olds has founded a number of nonprofit organizations that have had local and national impact. Two of his latest endeavors, the Midwest Minority Think Tank for Public Policy, Leadership, and Service, LLC. and the Midwest Minority Think Tank Foundation, LLC., were launched to serve the people in whatever realm that a conundrum may arise.

CONTACT DATA:

Blog: www.themidwestthinktank.com

Web Site: www.midwestminoritythinktank.com

Justice, Liberation & Salvation Youtube Channel:
https://www.youtube.com/channel/UCQF4Tr0bYyJ9s88uskvRC
HA

YouTube: Mark Carven Olds

Facebook: www.facebook.com/MarkCOlds

Twitter: https://twitter.com/midwestminority

Email: markcarvenolds@midwestminoritythinktank.com

Or   mcolds49@gmail.com

Cell: 216.389.4340

The Baedeker to Nationhood

Authored by: Mark Carven Olds, MNO

List Price: **$24.95 6" x 9"** (15.24 x 22.86 cm)
ISBN-13: 978-1517586560 ISBN-10: 1517586569 BISAC: Political Science / Political Ideologies / Democracy

The conundrum that will surround Nation Building can be found in the demystification of the programmatic intent. Nation Building will not threaten the people by coercion or the government with violence. Nation Building will sustain an ostracized people with hope and shall invoke a number of tangible economic endeavors as a methodology to lessen their dependence upon the existing system. Nationhood will help eliminate its citizenry from the welfare rolls, public housing subsidies, entitlement programs, and healthcare supplements. In addition, nationhood status will significantly help reduce the number of individuals on probation, parole, and confined in penal colonies. At the same time, nationhood will create entrepreneurial opportunities, build businesses, provide jobs, and reduce school dropout rates. Nationhood will also provide the illustration of covenant living through a Theocratic Interdependent Peaceful Society (T.I.P.S.).

The fast pace of everyday life can often remove the analytical process that may reduce the nationhood emergence to many as a complicated riddle or an impossible feat to produce. When the analysis has been applied to Nation Building as if to a job related initiative, personal involvement will then cause the view of systemic change to take on a more proportional advancement. In other words, it can be seen in smaller steps that will lead to a massive undertaken. However, the colossal venture of Nation Building will never seem doable to a people who have been cemented to only function in the current system.

CreateSpace eStore: https://www.createspace.com/5770775

Also Available: Amazon.com * Amazon Europe * Kindle * Bookstores and Online Retailers

A Complex Issue: (A Succinct Apothegmatic of Nation Building) Authored by Mr. Mark Carven Olds

List Price: **$24.95 6" x 9"** (15.24 x 22.86 cm)
Black & White on White paper 182 pages
ISBN-13: 978-1518754555 ISBN-10: 1518754554
BISAC: Political Science / Political Ideologies / General

Nationhood shall appear as a conundrum to the coeval elements of power; thus, evoking an automatic propaganda campaign to label the endeavor as disingenuous.

Nation Building will garner the attention of those designated to lower class status. The process shall call for an egression from the prevalent system.

A noncompliant attitude toward acceptance of an inferior position will signal the need for both economic and social recalibration. By an ongoing disparity practice of the wealth and resources of the world, nationhood status for the imperfect people and the impoverished people will present a predicament or quandary to the commerce arena as currently in universal practice. Up to this point, the imperfect people and the impoverished people have failed to control any industry domestically or globally. However, the practice of collective economics by them can re-arrange the methods that current industries exercise in the manner that they conduct commerce with the less fortunate.

Nation Building will reveal itself as a riddle, awaiting to be resolved by both the recipients of nationhood status and those who will vehemently oppose its mission.

When the Doctrine of Nation Building has been fully exposed to the multitudes who have been confined in the valley of decision, "the powers that be" and "the people in the valley" will seek a more transparent resolution. "The powers that be" will recognize a people have arrived at a strength that will demand change.